SONATINA

I

Printed in Great Britain

OXFORD UNIVERSITY PRESS, MUSIC DEPARTMENT, GREAT CLARENDON STREET, OXFORD OX2 6DP

Sonatina

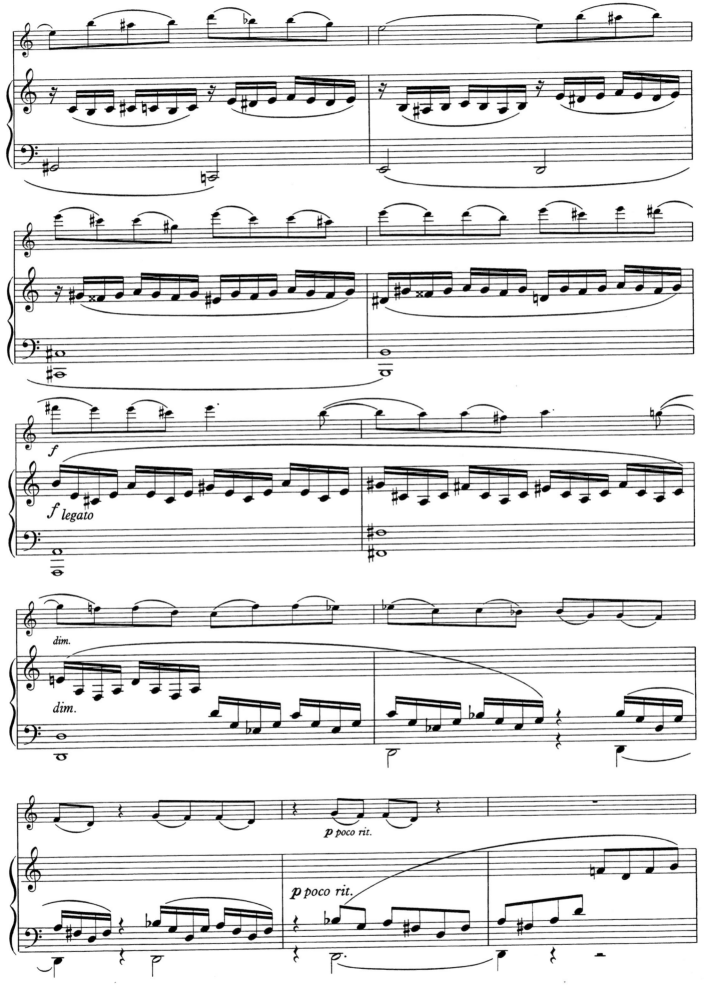

Sonatina

Sonatina

Sonatina

6

Sonatina

Sonatina

II

Andantino ($\quad$ = 63)

Sonatina

III

12

Sonatina

Sonatina

Sonatina

Sonatina

1956, revised 1961

Processed and printed by
Digital Books Logistics, Peterborough

Sonatina

OXFORD UNIVERSITY PRESS

Arnold Cooke

SONATINA
FOR FLUTE & PIANO

Oxford University Press

SONATINA

I

Flute

ARNOLD COOKE

Printed in Great Britain

OXFORD UNIVERSITY PRESS, MUSIC DEPARTMENT, GREAT CLARENDON STREET, OXFORD OX2 6DP

Sonatina

II

Andantino (♩ = 63)

III

Sonatina